BOSS MODE DECONSTRUCTED!

HOW THE DIABOLICAL GRIND CULTURE IS KILLING YOU and YOUR BUSINESS

Jessica AA Highsmith

Boss Mode Deconstructed: How the Diabolical Grind Culture is Killing You And Your Business

By Jessica AA Highsmith
© 2025 Empower Me Books | Urban-Executive Edition

No part of this book may be reproduced, stored in a retrieval system, or transmitted in any form or by electronic, mechanical, photocopying, recording, scanning, or otherwise, without the publisher's prior written permission.

Scripture taken from the New International Version (NIV). Copyright © 1973, 1978, 1984 by International Bible Society. Used by permission of Zondervan Publishing House. All rights reserved.

ISBN: 978-1954418356
Printed in the United States of America

First Edition: November 27, 2025

I dedicate this to every leader who's been crushed by the weight of performance, yet still chose purpose...

to those rebuilding from burnout, those navigating corporate spaces in the name of Kingdom assignments,

and those who ever thought they lost their footing; while yet learning, they were simply feeling the pressure of the Father's realignment.

BOSS MODE DECONSTRUCTED!

HOW THE DIABOLICAL GRIND CULTURE IS KILLING YOU and YOUR BUSINESS

Jessica AA Highsmith

Preface

There was a time when I thought the grind was holy. When I believed that if I just pushed harder, worked longer, showed up louder — God would somehow be more pleased with me. The world applauded my pace, but Heaven was grieved by my exhaustion. What I didn't realize was that I had started worshiping performance instead of walking in purpose.

Boss Mode Deconstructed, was birthed out of that collision. It was the moment when the strong one finally broke. When the "go-to" person in the office, the ministry, and the family finally sat still long enough to hear God whisper, *"I never told you to do all of that."*

This book isn't a resignation letter to ambition; it's a revelation about alignment. It's a reminder that obedience will always outperform overextension, that wisdom will always outrun workaholism, and that divine governance will always produce more fruit than human grind.

I wrote this for the high-performers and hidden servants that are called to the areas of healing and deliverance, who are called to the marketplace. It's for the professionals who pray in boardrooms and the prophets who manage deadlines. For the ones who know how to execute flawlessly, but have quietly lost the rhythm of grace, mercy and being soft and kind to yourself behind the noise of excellence.

You'll find yourself in these pages if you've ever:

- Felt unseen after giving everything.
- Been promoted publicly but depleted privately.
- Mistaken motion for meaning.
- Wanted to quit the assignment you once begged God for.

This is not just a leadership manual. It's a mirror, a mercy, and a map. A mirror that will show you where the hustle hijacked your heart. A mercy that will remind you that rest is still holy. And a map that will walk you back into divine strategy where your peace and your productivity are no longer enemies.

You'll laugh. You'll probably sigh. You might even cry. But by the end of it, you'll remember that you were never created to grind, you were created to govern. And governance looks like flow, not force. It looks like alignment, not anxiety. It looks like working from rest, not running on fumes. It looks like addressing overwhelm even when you weren't the one that brought it to your doorstep.

So, breathe again.
Lay down the heavy cape of self-reliance.
Pick up the mantle of stewardship.
And let's deconstruct the boss mode that culture built, so Heaven can rebuild the blueprint of who you really are.

— Jessica AA Highsmith
Urban-Executive Edition | Empower Me Books | Empower Me Enterprises

Introduction
The Mirage of Momentum

Hey BOSS! Did you even Notice? You've been bossing up so hard that your soul clocked out a long time ago!

Somewhere between the deadlines, the deliverables, and the digital applause, you started believing that motion meant progress. That as long as things were moving, something divine was happening.

But what happens when the motion is mechanical and not miraculous? What happens when your calendar is full, but your heart feels empty? What happens when you are told to rebrand yourself in an attempt to make you less of what the Father equipped to hand the Assignment. The rebrand stripped you of your necessary tools and God given "Spiritual Sense". You were desensitized, and now your discernment needs RECALIBRATION! You need to REST for this to happen. But NOT just in the natural sense of the word.

Let's be honest, we've all been there! Running off caffeine, purpose playlists, and prayer breaks; squeezed between back-to-back meetings. You keep saying, *"Once I finish this project, I'll rest."* But the project turns into a program, and the program turns into a lifestyle. Before long, you're managing the momentum but missing the meaning. Momentum is a masterful illusion! It convinces you that you're being productive when you're really just being busy. It disguises stress as success. It applauds activity but never asks about alignment. Culture taught us to *rise, grind, and slay.* But the Kingdom says, *rest, govern, and obey.* One is fueled by adrenaline; the other is sustained by anointing.

The danger is that adrenaline can feel like anointing when you've been overperforming for too long. That's why many leaders don't realize they're burned out — because they're still producing. They're still getting results, still leading teams, still showing up with excellence. But inwardly? They're drained. Numb. Quietly questioning if God still sees them.

The world calls it high-functioning burnout. Heaven calls it misalignment, operating outside of His Grace. Somewhere along the way, we equated worth with workload, visibility with value, and performance with purpose. But God never asked us to prove our worth; He asked us to *walk in it.*

In corporate spaces, I used to wear my exhaustion like an achievement badge. I believed that if I didn't show fatigue, people would assume I wasn't working hard enough. I had the data, the deliverables, and the decorum; but I didn't have peace. And when you've lost peace, you've already forfeited the promotion Heaven intended for that season.

That's when I learned: Heaven doesn't reward overextension; it honors obedience. I don't move by ambition. I move by aligned assignment. Because when you're aligned, grace governs your growth. When you're aligned, systems flow instead of fracture.

When you're aligned, you don't have to chase outcomes; outcomes start chasing *you.*

I wrote this book because I don't want you to learn that lesson the hard way. I want to teach you how to lead with rhythm, not rush. How to perform with peace, not pressure. How to manage excellence without mismanaging your emotional health.

We're going to expose the systems that celebrate overwork. We're going to confront the spirits behind exhaustion, manipulation, and false validation. We're going to talk about what happens when your body, your mind, and your spirit start waving the same white flag. We will also discuss how to rebuild before the burnout becomes bondage. You'll laugh, you'll reflect, you might even cry… but most importantly, you'll remember who you are!

You were never created to grind; you were created to govern. You were never called to chase applause; you were called to steward assignment. And you were never meant to survive the system; you were chosen to *reform* it.

So, if you're tired but still called, drained but still devoted, questioning but still chosen; welcome! Yes You, this is your safe place to pause, to breathe, and to realign. Because this isn't just another leadership reset.
This is your divine realignment.
Welcome to **Boss Mode Deconstructed !!**

FOREWORD

by B. Jacqueline Jeter
Boss Mode Deconstructed: How the Diabolical Grind Culture Is Killing You and Your Business

When I first encountered Jessica AA Highsmith's work, I immediately recognized a voice that carried both boardroom wisdom and Heaven's authority, an uncommon fusion of prophetic revelation and operational clarity that could only be forged in the fire of lived experience. Hers is not the voice of a theorist, nor the tone of someone pontificating from a distance, nor is it a passing trend dressed up in spiritual jargon. Jessica speaks as one who has walked the tightrope over burnout and breakthrough, who has stared down the barrel of soul-crushing corporate culture and emerged—not merely with survival tips, but with a divine blueprint for leaders who are tired of pretending that burnout is a badge of honor and a blueprint for true Kingdom governance.

In these pages, you will hear the rare harmony of prophetic insight and practical strategy. Jessica bridges what many dare not: the sacred and the secular, the sanctuary and the staff meeting, the prayer closet and the quarterly review. She has the audacity to ask hard questions: What if our exhaustion isn't noble but a symptom of disobedience? What if the very pace that wins applause in the marketplace is grieving the Spirit who called us to lead? Her life embodies these questions. She does not write from a distance, but from a live experience of the trenches of corporate boardrooms and the sanctuary of her own healing process. The Father forged this book through her tears, her breakthrough, and the radical recalibration that only comes from saying "enough" to the grind and "yes" to His governance.

Boss Mode Deconstructed arrives at a critical hour. Leaders in both the marketplace and ministry are suffocating beneath the seductive weight of performance, justifying it with sacred language while their souls quietly burn out. What makes this book even more timely is that we are living in an age where grind culture masquerades as greatness. Where ministry leaders brag about how little they sleep, and marketplace leaders quietly hemorrhage emotionally behind their metrics. The world hails hustle as holy; Jessica dares to call it what it is: the counterfeit of Kingdom order, a diabolical plot to disconnect sons and daughters from their original design. In a time when the illusion of momentum masquerades as progress, when busyness is mistaken for blessing, and when adrenaline is too often confused for anointing, Jessica's prophetic clarity refuses to leave the idols of performance unchallenged. This is a message for the CEO, the servant, the prophet, and the project manager. It is for anyone who has ever believed the lie that fruitfulness requires forfeiting wellness.

Jessica writes with the precision of a strategist and the compassion of a deliverance minister. She dissects the grind not simply as a productivity problem, but as a spiritual misalignment, a counterfeit that seduces leaders into believing they can outwork what God intended them to out-walk. Her revelation is sharp enough to pierce yet tender enough to heal. She challenges your pace, your patterns, and your perceptions, while simultaneously guiding you into a deeper intimacy with the One who called you.

Between these pages, leaders can prepare to lay down the trophies of exhaustion and pick up the mantle of rest. Leaders will find clarity about the difference between God-assigned work and self-imposed striving. They will find healing, as Jessica compassionately names the wounds that hustle culture normalizes. They will experience leadership recalibration, because this book retrains your instincts toward rest, discernment, and authority rooted in obedience, not overextension. Be prepared to laugh, sigh, even grieve what stress may have stolen, but expect, above all, an encounter of spiritual renewal, because Jessica brings them back to God's original model, governance, not grind, assignment, not addiction to achievement

This foreword is not merely an endorsement of a book so, dear reader, as you open these pages, let your guard down. As you engage these pages, I encourage you to do what leaders rarely give themselves permission to do, slow down. Breathe. Exhale the pressure. Allow Heaven to speak louder than your deadlines, to question your systems and strip away what is misaligned. Jessica has crafted not just content but a sanctuary, a place where fatigued professionals, weary leaders, intercessors in cubicles, prophets in boardrooms, and high-capacity servants can finally be honest about the cost of the pace they've been keeping.

You are holding more than wisdom; you are holding a divine strategy manual. It is a mirror for your motivation. Let every chapter challenge you, confront you, comfort you, and ultimately call you back home to the rhythm of grace.

As you turn the page, may your spirit become more attuned.
May your leadership become more intentional.
May your boundaries become holy.
And may your governance become prophetic, peaceful, and powerful.

I bless your journey through this book.
May every revelation bring realignment.

May every correction bring clarity.
May every truth bring transformation.

Because what you are about to read is not just insight, it is Heaven's blueprint written by a surrendered revolutionist for those ready to govern by grace, not grind.

Contents

Dedication

Preface
Introduction
Foreword — B. Jacqueline Jeter
    International Keynote Speaker & Trainer | Certified Leadership and Neuro Leader Coach | International Author | Women's Leadership Mentor | Breast Cancer Advocate | Clinical Research Scientist

---

Part I — The Breakdown: When Heaven Interrupts the Hustle

Chapter 1 — When Heaven Hires You
    Discovering purpose in the middle of pressure and redefining what "being called" really means in the workplace.

Chapter 2 — Flow Over Force: The Reset
    How burnout exposed the difference between grind and grace, and what it truly means to rest in divine alignment.

Chapter 3 — Flow vs. Force: When Grace Lifts
    Lessons from corporate disobedience, influence without authority, and what happens when Heaven says, "Exit."

Chapter 4 — Momentum Without Mayhem: D^3O Framework
    Delegation. Discernment. Divine Timing. Obedience.

Learning to steward high-capacity leadership without chaos.

Chapter 5 — The Cost of Clarity: Aligned Assignment vs. Ambition
When revelation requires separation and how to navigate pruning, boundaries, and purpose without losing peace.

Part II — The Flip: Culture vs. Kingdom

The world taught us to perform. Heaven taught us to abide.

Chapter 6 — Rise, Grind, Slay → Literally Killing Us
Exposing grind culture and teaching Kingdom leaders how to build systems that breathe.

Chapter 7 — The Know-Like-Trust Factor: When Familiarity Replaces Responsibility, Credibility & Authority
Deconstructing false authenticity, overexposure, and misplaced loyalty while reclaiming divine boundaries.

Chapter 8 — The Cost of Proving Yourself
The silent tax of overperformance and how to exit the proving stage with peace, evidence, and elevation.

Chapter 9 — Authenticity in Weakness: When Transparency Becomes a Weapon and a Witness
Healing through humility and learning how to lead while still being human.

Part III — The Blueprint: Healing the Leader Within

Chapter 10 — The Apostolic Charge: Gracious Mercy Over Grind
Reforming culture through governance, grace, and healing leadership rooted in Apostolic Resilience.

Final Author's Note

Epilogue — Cleared for Construction
A prophetic commissioning for builders, reformers, and Analytical Seers: restored, renewed, and ready to lead.

Afterword — Lillie A. Hill
Director | RN | Certified Wellness Coach | Corporate Speaker & Trainer

Acknowledgements
About the Author
Other Titles by Jessica AA Highsmith
Journal Pages for Notes

PART I

The Setup; Deconstructing the Hustle!

Chapter 1 — Boss Mode Deconstructed

In the beginning, work was worship. It wasn't warfare. It wasn't hustle and it for sure wasn't 60-hour weeks or 2 a.m. emails. That sort of ideology will literally take you strait to hell. In this case, I mean the grave. Stick with me and follow what I'm saying closely.

When God placed Adam in the garden, He didn't say *grind it till you make it.* He said, *"tend it and keep it."* (Gen. 2:15) That means cultivate and guard. Adam's assignment was to steward, not to strive. But once sin entered the picture, sweat became part of the story. The curse turned what was once graceful governance into grueling grind. That's why I tell people all the time: *the grind was never God's idea.* The grind is a by-product of disobedience and distraction. It's the evidence that somewhere, someone traded revelation for results.

Revelation, Resistance & Divine Reset

God never intended for His sons and daughters to earn what He already provided. He gave Adam authority before He gave him effort. Dominion came before deliverables. The same still applies to us... our titles, promotions, and metrics don't make us powerful; alignment does.

When I was moving through corporate systems, I thought excellence required exhaustion. I thought authority came from access and performance. So, I did what most of us do — I over-prepared, over-produced, and over-proved. And the Lord kept whispering, *"You're operating under the curse, not the covenant."* My Boss would say, "You are suffering from Imposter Syndrome" and then try to gaslight me into believing that I wasn't doing my job well enough, excellent enough, or giving enough. You BETTER KNOW who you are. Who are you Adam? Where art thou??? Smile with me, now laugh!

Culture glamorizes the curse. It hands out applause for burnout and trophies for trauma. In the corporate world, if you're not tired, people assume you're not serious. In ministry, if you rest, people accuse you of losing fire. We've baptized busyness and called it devotion. We've confused "faithful" with "frantic." But Heaven measures success differently. Heaven's metric is obedience.

A few years back, I had a mentee that the Lord gave me a word that resonates for this same space. There won't be another word given outside of the first word I already gave. In other words, Did you obey the 1st word? The first instruction? And obedience often looks like slowing down long enough to hear the next instruction. Her word was for ME TOO!!!

When I finally allowed God to deconstruct my own boss mode, He walked me back through Genesis. *"Jessica, I gave humanity six days of authority and one day of absence; and you're trying to lead all seven.* "That hit me hard. Because I realized that grind culture doesn't just steal energy; it steals intimacy. If the enemy can keep you constantly producing, he can keep you from perceiving, discerning, hearing, resting in Abba.

That's when I started rebuilding my rhythm. II had found myself doing the mindless Facebook Scroll. Aggravated and just trying to get away from it all for a moment and it became a norm for a season smh. I had to get back to my previous state of scheduling *Selah Moments* into my week — pauses where I'd literally close the laptop, silence the phone, and ask, *"God, what are we doing, not what am I doing?"* I shared at the *'2024 Literary Celebration of Miracles: Chayil Women BE WEALTHY'* where I would schedule myself breaks on my calendar. It was often in those spaces where clarity would show up. Projects got easier. Teams flowed better. Even my creativity would be refreshed by the Central Processing of Holy Spirit. *Laugh*

The Reform

The new boss mode isn't about domination; it's about **delegation, discernment, divine timing, AND Obedience**. I call it D^3O. Laughing out Loud (lol)! I was a Chemist by training, so of course I'm going to turn this acronym into a Molecule. Think of it as a Spiritual

Framework that was derived strait from out of Compton. Just kidding. The Bible, duh!

It's understanding that leadership was never meant to cost you your peace. You can be called, competent, and calm at the same time. You can meet deadlines without dying inside. You can deliver excellence without surrendering essence.

Every leader needs to ask:

"Am I cultivating the garden God gave me, or am I trying to plow a field He never assigned OR Did IIIIIIIII change the assignment?" Because if you're grinding in a place you were only meant to govern, you're living beneath your design.

 Real Talk Reflection:

- Where have I mistaken the curse of grind for the calling to govern?

 Shift Statement:

- I was never created to grind; I was created to govern with grace.

 Activation Exercise:

- Audit your current assignments. Identify one task, meeting, or expectation that feels heavy but hasn't been authorized by God.

Pause it for seven days and watch how alignment restores energy.

Chapter 2 — The Diabolical Agenda of Hustle Culture

Let's go ahead and call it what it is … the hustle has an agenda!

And No Ma'am, No Sir, I'm not talking about your brand strategy or quarterly goals. I'm talking about the spiritual system behind burnout. The invisible infrastructure that convinces high-performing believers that busyness equals blessing.

Hustle culture isn't just a mindset; it's a manipulative mechanism designed to disconnect you from rest, redefine your worth, and distort your discernment. It tells you that your "yes" must always be immediate, your calendar must always be full, and your phone must always be on.

Well let me tell you, my phone is Automatically set to DO NOT DISTURB at 8 pm EST. EVERY NIGHT! And has been for years, but yet, I still have to monitor my own guard rails! Make no mistake, hustle is hell's counterfeit for Holy momentum.

The Revelation

The enemy doesn't have to get you to sin if he can get you to strive. If he can keep you exhausted, he can keep you ineffective. If he can keep you performing, he can keep you from perceiving. And that's exactly what happened to me. There was a time when unconsciously I believed that exhaustion meant excellence. I knew in my mind that this wasn't true. I knew biblically that it wasn't true; but my actions started doing something else without my even having noticed. I was sending messages that I never intended to even send. My staying late started to look like loyalty in all the wrong ways.

My working through lunch proved started to look like a level of dedication that I never even planned to give. The truth? I had subconsciously made work an idol because fatigue had become familiar.

And here's the thing, fatigue should have never even been there in the first place. When you get distracted, lullabied, and off assignment, you become exhausted. You become a functional drunk spiritually. To be spiritual sober simply means you still feel the Holy Spirit's nudge before you reply, schedule, or sign; it's awareness anchored in obedience. I'm told that one of my natural parents struggled with Alcohol. So, this is just a natural example that helped me understand this principle.

When I lost spiritual sobriety the enemy could attack all systems through every cracked window!!! And Guess what, you don't have to be "unhealed" necessarily for that to happen. You can just be burned out from a *doing well* — from *well-doing*!!! <u>Catch It !</u>

Shaking My Head. Yep!

I've found myself in both places on different occasions. What I will tell you is that both the brokenness of burnout and the weariness of over-performance can leave you wide open if you don't guard your spirit.

Every spreadsheet was strategic, but none of it was *spiritual*. Every deliverable had data, but no divine direction. I had become so accustomed to being efficient that I forgot how to be *led*.

And that's the diabolical part. Hustle disguises itself as purpose. It rewards production while quietly bankrupting your peace. It gives you visibility while robbing you of vision. It's what I call the Eve Effect ... when the enemy uses partial truth to provoke premature action. Or the enemy plays mental games and tells you how you have done ALL these things for the sake of the assignment and shows you ALL the ways in which you are being robbed. It's the Eve Effect. He Never shows you that, the thing you think no one knows was stolen from you has been accounted for by Heaven.

He doesn't show you the vessels or instruments that God is using to mention your name and work in rooms you've yet to step in and that you don't need to strive or even give space to the gas-lighting that's coming from that superior.

All you need to do is the [Assignment]{.underline} that the Father gave you. Nothing more, Nothing Less! That Is Excellence! Imagine that. NOTHING ELSE. This is NOT a punishment. It's a test. Jesus was tested in the same way, don't fail. Excellence is not punishment; it's obedience on display.

The Resistance

Culture will applaud you while you die quietly. Corporate systems will hand you plaques for your performance while ignoring the price you paid to produce it. They will clap for your metrics, not your mental health. They will repackage the work you did and call it innovation and swear that it was only a fluke that you were able to do it. You will either get angry *(I did)*; or if you're not careful, you'll start clapping too. Either way — for the very thing that's draining you. That's how quick the enemy will try to attack you (oppress) with the Leviathan Spirit. It seeks to twist the perspective on the Assignment that the Father gave you and make sure you place your focus on the Narrative that it has created vs the one the Father gave you. You knew the instructions.

I didn't start clapping but I did get upset with the notion that I somehow wasn't "smart enough" or good enough to get it right the first time. I was angry because every time I delivered, that same response came back; silence, dismissal, or repackaging. But that wasn't pride; that was the ache of being misunderstood in a space God had already validated me. There's a difference between ego and evidence.

Pride demands recognition, but obedience is often mistaken for arrogance.

Let's talk about what's really happening. So you will identify it like I had to with the Father. Hustle culture was built to feed insecurity. It keeps people in a cycle of proving instead of *partnering* with God. I have from the beginning of my business always said that I am CO-Partners with Holy Spirit of Empower Me Enterprises, Inc and Empower Me Books and the Founder of Empowered to Heal Ministries International. Why is this important???? Because in the same way that I recognized this in my business, we must also REMAIN this way while we work, serve and lead in the marketplace. In this instance Corporate America.

I was NOT Co-Partnering with Corporate. I was STILL supposed to CO-partner with Holy Spirit. If you miss this principle and Revelation Key, you will start saying "yes" to opportunities that were **never** assignments. You will Stay too long. You start equating access with favor, when sometimes it's just distraction wearing a designer suit.

That's what happened to me when I stayed longer than I was supposed to in that corporate environment. God had already told me the assignment was complete, but I kept signing up for new projects... not because He said stay, but because I didn't want to look like I was quitting a hard or difficult assignment. In the beginning God had in fact told me *"3,"* and I was trying to determine if that 3 was months or years. A couple of Apostolic and Prophetic mentors I sought counsel with helped me determine that the '3' was 3-years. I gained confirmation in prayer.

All you need to do is the [Assignment]{.underline} that the Father gave you. Nothing more, Nothing Less! That Is Excellence! Imagine that. NOTHING ELSE. This is NOT a punishment. It's a test. Jesus was tested in the same way, don't fail. Excellence is not punishment; it's obedience on display.

The Resistance

Culture will applaud you while you die quietly. Corporate systems will hand you plaques for your performance while ignoring the price you paid to produce it. They will clap for your metrics, not your mental health. They will repackage the work you did and call it innovation and swear that it was only a fluke that you were able to do it. You will either get angry *(I did)*; or if you're not careful, you'll start clapping too. Either way — for the very thing that's draining you. That's how quick the enemy will try to attack you (oppress) with the Leviathan Spirit. It seeks to twist the perspective on the Assignment that the Father gave you and make sure you place your focus on the Narrative that it has created vs the one the Father gave you. You knew the instructions.

I didn't start clapping but I did get upset with the notion that I somehow wasn't "smart enough" or good enough to get it right the first time. I was angry because every time I delivered, that same response came back; silence, dismissal, or repackaging. But that wasn't pride; that was the ache of being misunderstood in a space God had already validated me. There's a difference between ego and evidence.

Pride demands recognition, but obedience is often mistaken for arrogance.

Let's talk about what's really happening. So you will identify it like I had to with the Father. Hustle culture was built to feed insecurity. It keeps people in a cycle of proving instead of *partnering* with God. I have from the beginning of my business always said that I am CO-Partners with Holy Spirit of Empower Me Enterprises, Inc and Empower Me Books and the Founder of Empowered to Heal Ministries International. Why is this important???? Because in the same way that I recognized this in my business, we must also REMAIN this way while we work, serve and lead in the marketplace. In this instance Corporate America.

I was NOT Co-Partnering with Corporate. I was STILL supposed to CO-partner with Holy Spirit. If you miss this principle and Revelation Key, you will start saying "yes" to opportunities that were **never** assignments. You will Stay too long. You start equating access with favor, when sometimes it's just distraction wearing a designer suit.

That's what happened to me when I stayed longer than I was supposed to in that corporate environment. God had already told me the assignment was complete, but I kept signing up for new projects... not because He said stay, but because I didn't want to look like I was quitting a hard or difficult assignment. In the beginning God had in fact told me *"3,"* and I was trying to determine if that 3 was months or years. A couple of Apostolic and Prophetic mentors I sought counsel with helped me determine that the '3' was 3-years. I gained confirmation in prayer.

The enemy used an issue that I *used to think I had*. I thought I would run away from problems because someone "SPOKE it and I accepted it as TRUE". It was in fact untrue. It had been spoken by someone that was a master manipulator. Just like a battered woman should NOT remain in an abusive house, I knew that and I would allow myself to be gaslight to please people, to prove them wrong when I was very young. This thing I realized is used and was used often as council with me sometimes just from friends and family that desired me to not keep experiencing the toxicity.

I had to hear God and OBEY the FIRST instruction. here's what I learned: *when Heaven releases you, staying is disobedience disguised as dedication...it will result in a SPIRITUAL DEATH and can lead to a PHYSICAL ONE!*

The Reset

The reset came when God made me slow down long enough to see the pattern. Every time I stayed in a place past its expiration date, my peace evaporated. Every time I tried to meet people's expectations more than His instructions, something inside me broke; spiritually, emotionally, and physically.

When the physical symptoms appeared—the fatigue, the weakness, the pain—that's when revelation hit: the grind had graduated from mental to spiritual warfare to physical attacks on my health to an **ONSLAUGHT.** My body was revealing what my spirit had been suppressing.

Now, let me clarify something. Manifested warfare is a <u>demonic</u> <u>attack</u>, but that doesn't always mean you're <u>oppressed</u>. *Sometimes Heaven allows pressure so you can see what's still unguarded*. It's not always punishmen; it can be protection and preparation.

During that same season—what later became *The 40-Day Onslaught*—I was physically attacked yet again, by a spirit of infirmity; while some around me misread it as a "python" or "divination" spirit.

In reality, my body was under siege, my spirit man was fighting off attacks. I was medically burned out and spiritually exposed, and the wrong word was spoken into open cracks.

In that same season, someone spoke a word over me while I was already exhausted and spiritually porous. I didn't realize how open the cracks had become until infirmity walked right through them in. That's what happens when burnout meets misplaced words—you become susceptible to spirits that would've never had legal access if rest and boundaries were intact. It wasn't divination; it was depletion. The enemy doesn't always need invitation—sometimes he just needs exhaustion. And when exhaustion <u>opens a window</u>, infirmity gladly walks through it.

That experience taught me to discern the difference between *prophetic insight* and *premature accusation*. True discernment partners with compassion; false discernment partners with condemnation and sometimes true discernment partners that just *Missed It*. If you've ever been mislabeled or misunderstood while you were suffering, go back and read *The 40-Day Onslaught*.

It gives the full context of that battle and the miracle of how God used it to reset my life.

From that moment on, I learned that the enemy doesn't always need an invitation; sometimes he only needs your exhaustion. And Heaven's antidote to exhaustion is not more striving; it's rest.

The real reset began when I stopped asking, *"What's next?"* and started asking, *"What's necessary?"* Because just because something is requested or just because you are asked to do it at your job or by your client, doesn't mean it is for you to do. Nor does this mean its aligned with the actual assignment.

The Reform

So, here's the new rhythm, I don't grind, I govern. I don't hustle, I honor Heaven's timing. I don't move for validation, I move via radical obedience. This reform isn't just personal—it's prophetic. It's a restoration of the Garden mandated revelation: to tend, to keep, and to walk with God in the cool of the day. A Revelation that God gave me in Feb 2025 as I prepared to deliver part I of this word to the Junior League of Orange County on behalf of an invitation from Dr. Danielle Robinson, PhD. You are now able to enjoy and benefit from this word today!

It's time to stop letting your job title dictate your joy. Stop letting your inbox or your boss be your idol. Stop letting productivity replace presence. Because the truth is this, you can't pour revelation from a weary vessel. You can't hear strategy when you're surviving on survival mode. And you can't reform systems that you're *still enslaved* to. So, here's your assignment rest before you reset. I did. Truthfully, I'm still on rest mode from Corporate America as I pen this book; because rest isn't weakness—it's obedience whether in warfare, worship or wilderness.

I choose flow over force, presence over performance, rest over rush.

―――――

 Real Talk Reflection:
- Where have I confused productivity with purpose, or busyness with blessing?

 Shift Statement:
- I refuse to glorify grind culture; I align with Heaven's cadence.

 Activation Exercise:
- Write down three activities or habits that keep you "busy but unfulfilled."

- Ask God to show you which ones were never assigned, and this week start saying *no* where He already released you.

Chapter 3 — Flow vs. Force

Sometimes Heaven gives you a strategy that only works if everyone involved chooses alignment, and when they don't, you learn the painful difference between *flow* and *force*.

I learned that lesson through a project called ChangePoint® Integration. On paper, it was brilliant: a governance system that could unify data, streamline reporting, and bring multiple departments into rhythm. God had downloaded the vision, the sequence, even the change-management approach. The only missing piece was agreement.

But instead of alignment, I met resistance.

The Revelation

The only way that project could have succeeded was if the site's senior leadership came into unity with the strategy Heaven had handed me. I could lay out the blueprint, communicate the why, and present the path forward; but I couldn't make them walk it.

That's where most leaders get trapped. We think revelation equals responsibility for other people's obedience. But flow stops the moment you start forcing what only humility can fix.

They wanted to terminate an external consultant—someone whose short-term contract would have cost them millions and hand me the entire workload instead for a mid-level rate. "Influence without authority," they called it. Translation: *You build it, test it, write it, govern it, tolerate the disrespect we excuse in no one else, and do it all quietly.*

Every line of that assignment screamed *force.* Heaven's agenda never intended for me to be exploited. When grace lifts, even your brilliance becomes heavy.

The Reset

Eventually, exhaustion became my teacher. I could feel Heaven whisper, *"You are carrying the weight of a system I never asked you to sustain." I never even asked YOU to build it. I asked you to deliver the Strategy, and to lead the effort and serve and teach where necessary.*

If I had left when I was supposed to, I would have remained at the head of the assignment—still in divine order, still operating in authority. Instead, I stayed, and the assignment turned on me.

That's what happens when *grace expires, but guilt keeps you working*. You go from stewarding to striving. From governing to grinding. From divine partnership to forced performance. Guilt for something that didn't belong to me. I took on shame that was unjustly applied to me." → "I carried guilt for something that didn't belong to me—shame unjustly applied."

The project that once carried God's breath started draining mine. And I learned that no amount of strategic brilliance can resurrect a season Heaven has buried. When the ask shifts from Heaven's intent to human exploitation, obedience means exit.

I should have shaken the dust from my feet and trusted the Father as my source. But I kept forcing movement where there was no flow. The result? Burnout, betrayal, and the realization that I had stepped *out of grace*—still talented, but tired; still gifted, but grieved.

The Reform

Flow doesn't require fighting. It simply requires faith, timing, and trust. Force manipulates outcomes. Flow is manifested by God and is always in order. Force demands results on your timeline. Flow produces fruit in God's. I had to be okay with KNOWING I had done all that I was SUPPOSED to do for a company that wanted to force something that God was saying I was now released from. I had to relearn that my job was never to make things happen. It was to stay available when Heaven decided to move. My responsibility was *response,* not *control.*

Now I gauge every assignment by its <u>ease of grace</u>: If peace is absent, I pause. If flow dries up, I step back. If results require manipulation, I check alignment before I am manipulated by shallow and deathly applause.

That's how you discern whether you're flowing or forcing. One is led by grace; the other is led by guilt. One multiplies, the other drains. One honors God's timing and governance; the other rushes ahead or disregards council and calls it leadership or executive decisions.

— — — — —

 Real Talk Reflection:
- Where have you been forcing what Heaven has already lifted? Are you trying to sustain an assignment that no longer carries grace?

 Shift Statement:
- I release every season I've been trying to keep alive by my own effort. I choose flow over force, trust over tension, peace over pressure.

 Activation Exercise:
- Write down one project, relationship, or responsibility that currently feels heavy.

- **Ask God:** "Is this still mine?"
- If you sense He's released you, stop forcing it.
- Replace striving with stillness this week and let the proof of flow, peace, return. Do you see a 100-fold return on your investment or are you bankrupt?

Chapter 4 — Momentum Without Mayhem: The D³O Framework

Sometimes The decrees of heaven's throne room slows you down not because you're unqualified, but because you're over-carrying. You ever over-carried, lol? I did—with my youngest child, formerly baby Noah!

That's what I mean by *Momentum Without Mayhem*—the ability to move with divine velocity without losing your internal peace. It's forward motion that doesn't fracture you. It's progress powered by presence. Heaven's kind of momentum doesn't require panic, pressure, or proving; it requires rhythm, restraint, and rest. When God's hand is on your pace, even your pauses are productive; so yes, that tv binge of Season '*whatever*', is also included!

You prayed for elevation but then refused to let go of everything that came with the last season. You delegated tasks, but not trust. You moved in discernment but still tried to manage the outcome.

You said "yes" to divine timing but scheduled it according to your calendar. Whew Jesus! I'll raise my hand! It was me Lord; lol!

That's when God started teaching me what I now call **D³O — Delegation, Discernment, Divine Timing, and Obedience.** Remember from Chapter 1. It's not just a leadership framework; it's Heaven's way of helping high-capacity people pace their purpose. Listen I grew up having trouble remembering current things because my mind was busy storing ALL the things I and the Lord deemed important; lol. Frameworks are a thing the Father and my 'Adoptive Real Mother' must have instilled in me. Now, it's how he sometimes teaches me things that he expects ME to remember, and I therefore now share them as he leads with those I lead, serve, admonish etc. Yes, 'Adoptive Real Mother' is an oxymoron lol, joke intended

The Revelation

After I finally walked away from that corporate assignment, I expected instant breakthrough. I thought that since I had obeyed, everything would move fast, new contracts, new clarity, new clients. But Heaven had something else in mind, *a pause*.

He told me, *"You moved when I said move, but now I need you to learn how to move at My speed."*

Divine timing is the rhythm of revelation. You can't rush it, replicate it, or re-engineer it. I told y'all I was a trained Chemist and process engineer. Partner that with Holy Spirit calling me a Nabi and Seer and my goodness I had to learn to go at HIS pace. My pace is lightning speed lol.

God started unpacking each part of D³O.

Delegation
Stop trying to be the entire body when you're only called to be one part. True stewardship requires trust. Heaven doesn't promote control freaks; it promotes conduits.

I know, I know, You may be like Jess, I can hear you, but what do I do when it's not me refusing to delegate—when there's literally no one to hand it to, or when those who could help refuse to step up?

I've been there. You're carrying a load that was supposed to be shared, and you're doing it out of obedience, not ego. The team is under-resourced. Leadership isn't listening. And now, the same excellence that once opened doors has become the excuse for why they won't give you help.

In moments like that, delegation becomes *spiritual,* not structural. You start by delegating to **God first.** This is why systems are important! Systems were first, heaven ordained before any business or corporation could comprehend the term. All you need to do is hand Him, the Father, the part that's breaking you while you continue to steward the part He's assigned.

It sounds simple, but it's warfare. Heaven never intended for you to substitute submission with self-sufficiency. When help doesn't show up in people, it often shows up in *process.* God will teach you to streamline, to simplify, and to say no. He'll give you strategy to cut the clutter until the help He promised arrives. I promise, I'm having to implement this like you.

So yes, delegate, even if no one's available. Delegate the burden to Heaven. Delegate the outcomes to grace. Delegate your exhaustion to rest. *Because if you carry what only God can sustain, you'll collapse under the illusion of competence.*

Discernment
Everything good isn't God. The enemy disguises distractions as "urgent opportunities." You need divine filters, not just professional foresight.

Divine Timing
Delay doesn't mean denial. Sometimes God slows down your plans so He can speed up your preparation.

Obedience
Obedience is the currency of elevation. Every new dimension requires *a fresh "yes" without negotiation.*

These four elements have become my internal governance system. They are teaching me that miracles have management structures!

The Reset

Even after leaving corporate life, I realized hustle had a residue. I was still trying to out-perform silence. I'd catch myself over-committing, thinking productivity equaled purpose.

God would whisper, *"Jessica, you're delegating projects but not pressure."* I had to unlearn the instinct to do everything myself just because I could. **Delegation wasn't about getting help; it was about giving Heaven room to flow through others.**

Discernment started sharpening again when I stopped filling my schedule with busywork. I began to recognize what peace actually felt like—and that peace is proof of presence. Then came divine timing. I watched doors I could've forced open suddenly swing wide with no effort. The same people who overlooked me before started calling. That's the fruit of waiting well.

And obedience? That's the glue. You can have perfect timing, strong teams, and prophetic strategy; but without obedience, you'll still miss Heaven's target. Obedience keeps you aligned when logic tries to take the lead. If they are worried about the Key Performance Indicator (KPI), let them take it up with Jesus. I've found that when you are Kingdom aligned, the number ends up aligning with YOU aka your Heavenly Obedience.

The Reform

Now I live by the **D^3O rhythm:**
- **Delegate** what drains your grace.
- **Discern** what deserves your energy.
- Wait for *Divine timing* instead of demanding your own.
- **Obey** *in the Pressure*, even when you don't understand.

This is not a productivity hack; it's a preservation principle. *Because I was literally dying!*

When I implemented D³O, I stopped living in constant crisis management. My creativity returned. My body started to heal. I could breathe again. Heaven began showing me that divine flow always contains divine order. You can't expect Kingdom results using chaotic systems. As a Nabi & Seer, I tend to over-monitor my emotional intelligence at times. Therefore now, before I commit to anything, I run it through the D³O lens:

- Does this require delegation?
- Is my discernment clear or cloudy?
- Is this the right time, or just the right idea?
- And am I obeying—or over-analyzing?

If any answer breaks the rhythm, I pause, because in the Kingdom, pace is proof. Because at the end of the day, momentum without mayhem isn't about moving fast. It's about moving faithfully, in step with the One who authors both the pace *and* the purpose.

— — — — —

── **Real Talk Reflection:**
- Where have I been moving faster than grace or slower than obedience?

- What am I still carrying that someone else, or Heaven was meant to handle?

 Shift Statement:
- I choose to lead by revelation, not reaction.
- I release the need to force timing, control outcomes, or manage everything alone.

 Activation Exercise:
1.) Write out one current goal or project.
2.) Apply the D³O filter to it:

- What can be delegated?
- What needs discernment?
- What is Heaven's timing on this?
- What step of obedience is required next?

3.) Circle the one area that feels hardest to surrender and practice releasing it this week.

Chapter 5 — Aligned Assignment vs. Ambition: The Cost of Clarity

Once you've learned to flow, rest, and lead by divine rhythm, the next stage is *clarity,* and clarity always costs something. It costs relationships, titles, comfort, and sometimes identity. But it will never cost more than the abundance you gain through *radical obedience*. Because every divine exchange carries reward.

In surrendering what was temporary, you gain what is eternal; prosperous relationships, God-ordained partnerships, His peace, and substance that outweighs status or titles. You gain your true identity. Yes, even if you are called to the marketplace.

That's the difference between **Aligned Assignment** vs. **Ambition**. Ambition will have you chasing opportunities God never called you to; aligned assignment will have opportunities chasing *you.* Ambition feeds performance; alignment births peace. And I had to learn—sometimes the hard way—that even what the world coins as good ambition can become rebellion when it outruns obedience.

The Pruning After the Promotion

When I finally walked away from corporate, I expected peace to feel like palm trees and worship music. Instead, it felt like pruning shears. Heaven was cutting everything I'd used to prop myself up in the last season; the false stability, the familiar validation, the people who liked the *version* of me that fit their narrative. At first, I called it loss. But God called it clarity. It wasn't as if He had told me that I wasn't to go back. But if he ever sent me back, things would be drastically different. This was not the first time God had pulled me out prior to an elevation. You'll Have to read *A Superhero Ain't Nothing But a Sandwich*, the adult edition for that account.

Clarity doesn't coddle; it confronts. It holds up a mirror and says, *"This can't go with you."* I remember sitting one morning with my *Bolthouse Farms Green Juice* and realizing that half the relationships I was grieving were never covenant; they were convenience. They existed because of what I could *produce,* not who I actually was. That realization stung, but it freed me.

Revelation Requires Separation

Clarity doesn't just show you what's ahead; it exposes what's no longer aligned. When Heaven upgrades your sight, it also upgrades your boundaries. There were people I loved deeply who simply couldn't perceive me in my next dimension. Some thought my obedience was arrogance. Others interpreted my silence as shade. But Heaven wasn't isolating me; it was insulating me.

The clearer my vision became, the quieter my circle got. And God whispered via a close leader to me, *"You're not being left out; you're being set apart."* That's when I realized: I had been confusing ambition for assignment.

Ambition tells you to prove it; assignment tells you to steward it. Ambition fights for visibility; assignment flows in validity. Ambition chases crowds; assignment cultivates covenant. I had not confused *ambition* with *assignment*.

I had simply started walking out the *world's version* of success from a place of weariness. I was tired, stretched, and still trying to be faithful, but little by little I began operating in corporate patterns Heaven never authorized. It wasn't rebellion; it was *fatigue disguised as focus*.

Ambition didn't seduce me; *survival did*. And that's what happens when you're loyal to purpose but low on oil; you start performing principles without presence. Heaven had to remind me that alignment isn't about perfection; it's about pace. God wasn't rebuking me; He was realigning me.

Clarity teaches you that everyone can't be covenant. Some are assignments, some are seasons, and a few are destiny partners. Knowing the difference will save you unnecessary heartbreak. And yes, it hurts to discern that difference.

When you're wired to serve, build and lead, you want to take everyone with you. But obedience sometimes means walking alone long enough for God to re-introduce you as healed, whole, and holy.

The Reset

Clarity will break your heart before it blesses your life. It exposes your motives, your dependencies, and your distractions. It shows you where your loyalty has turned into idolatry. After I left, I struggled with silence. I kept asking God, *"Why did you remove them? Why did you close that door? Why does this obedience feel like exile?"*

He said, *"Because sight without separation creates sabotage."* In other words, you can't see clearly if you're still surrounded by people invested in your blindness. The pruning was protection. It was preparation for a new kind of partnership; not rooted in performance, but in purpose.

This was where my earlier lesson, D^3O, came alive again. **Discernment** showed me what to release. And IS STILL showing me. **Divine timing** keeps me from *replacing* what God removed. And **obedience** required me to *stay silent until the fruit spoke* for itself.

The Reform

Clarity births boundaries. Boundaries birth order. And order births abundance. Now I no longer chase crowds; I curate covenant. I never chased crowds; I actually ran from platforms unless it was the one God built for me. Heck, to think of it, that probably the only thing I've ever really ran from the most, until I finally just didn't lol.

Now, I simply curate covenant. I don't confuse proximity with purpose, or applause with affirmation.

I've learned that isolation for incubation isn't abandonment; it's alignment. It's how Heaven hides you long enough to heal you and prepare you for the stage that can hold your weight.

When you honor the cost of clarity, Heaven trusts you with greater responsibility because you've proven you won't idolize the wrong thing again. That's when the *right* people start appearing; the builders, the believers, the ones who don't need a résumé to recognize your anointing. They find you because you're finally positioned where God planted you.

Clarity has a cost, yes, but it also carries a *compounding return, that means the obedience of your harvest will pay you dividends*. <u>Baby</u>, <u>that's</u> <u>EXTRA!</u> I love me some bonus residuals. It pays you back in peace, in precision, and in partnerships that multiply purpose. So don't fear the pruning. Fear staying attached to what no longer grows.

— — — — —

Real Talk Reflection:
- Where has clarity revealed attachments I need to release?
- Who or what have I been trying to carry into a season they were never called to sustain?

Shift Statement:
- I embrace the cost of clarity because it preserves the call.
- I trade comfort for conviction and choose alignment over approval.

 Activation Exercise:
1.) Make a list of relationships, roles, or routines that feel heavy or out of sync.
2.) Ask Holy Spirit: *Is this pruning or is this partnership?*
3.) For everything He marks as pruning, bless it, release it, and stop rehearsing its absence.
   (Maybe I'm the ONLY one that does this.)
4.) For what remains, steward it well; don't fumble it, because the remnant will reproduce.

Part II

Culture vs. A Theocratic Mindset in the Marketplace Arenas

The marketplace is where Heaven's Culture and Earth's Systems collide. One demands performance. The other calls for presence. This section unveils how to reform, not just survive, those arenas through apostolic insight, prophetic governance, and practical leadership rhythm.

Chapter 6 — Rise, Grind, Slay
→ Literally Killing Us

The marketplace is where Heaven's culture and earth's systems **contend**—one demands performance, the other calls for presence." Only thing is, we don't' contend in the traditional sense — we **speak and build**. Why fight for something you already gained the victory in?

In the marketplace there is an *exchange*. We serve and lead the assignment based on *Heaven's Orders,* BUT we also gain understanding of the enemy's culture blueprint and then we build *Kingdom's Theocratic Strategy* on earth, exactly as it was seen, heard, and spoken in Heaven.

That's the real battle plan. Not fists. Not force. **Formation**. If you are called to lead and serve in the Marketplace in any capacity especially as Kingdom Strategist, Pioneer, or Influencer—someone called to operate within secular systems while carrying divine governance—then understand this: You will be sent into industries that worship grind culture like it's a god. Your job is not to mimic it.

Your job is to **model the rhythm of not just** *rest and revelation* but of Kingdom Dominion and Authority in the Earth.

The Revelation:
How Culture Corrupts Systems

Let's talk about what this looks like in real time:

→ **Pharma:** You're managing multimillion-dollar compliance projects under leadership that equates urgency with excellence. Every meeting is a fire drill, and deliverables are weaponized as validation. When racism or bias creeps in—subtle comments about how you "speak so well" or being consistently left out of decision rooms—you don't react in flesh; you respond with governance. You document. You protect the assignment. You stay postured in prayer and legally wise. *Because Heaven doesn't promote panic—it promotes protocol.*

→ **Banking:** You may sit under executives who mask greed as "strategy." The grind looks glamorous—bonuses, awards, power lunches—but underneath, people are spiritually bankrupt. When sexism shows up—when a male peer takes credit for your presentation or interrupts your voice—you don't compete, you **consecrate.** You release the outcome to God while documenting, following due process, and positioning yourself in excellence. *Favor is your force field. Strategy is your sword.*

→ **Construction / Engineering:** You might face blatant ageism—being overlooked because they assume your creativity has "timed out" or your youth means you "don't understand the field." The temptation will be to over-perform to prove worth. **Don't.** The Kingdom response is *consistency with conviction.* Keep receipts, contracts and justification logs when working in secular and business led environments (*proof in the earth is wisdom and prudence*), build systems that outlast opinions, and let the results testify. *Because Kingdom leaders don't chase validation… they steward evidence.*

→ **Healthcare:** The toxicity can be masked as "urgency for patient care." You're working twelve-hour shifts while someone else manipulates the narrative, stealing your solutions and lying about your workload. Executives know, but politics protects them. You could let anger speak, or you can let wisdom build. Establish boundaries, gather facts, *maintain decorum*, and keep a parallel paper trail. *Don't fight their lies with noise. Fight it with prayer, presence, records, rest, and revelation.*

The Reset:
The Answer Is Not to Do More

The answer is **not** to outwork them. It's not to wake up earlier, skip meals, and pour another cup of ambition pretending it's anointing. The answer is to CONTINUE to **rise in prayer** and to stand still and let God download *Heaven's next move.*

The most dangerous leaders in grind culture aren't the lazy ones...*they're the spiritually deaf ones.* When you stop listening, you start losing...even if the numbers say otherwise. Your assignment is to remain poised and resolute. Operate from rest, not rush. And when opposition arises, you know, the racism, sexism, gaslighting, exploitation, etc. Don't respond emotionally; respond structurally.

Use the **natural laws** of the land to support the **spiritual ones.** Know your HR policies. Understand your rights. Use your documentation wisely. And after you've done all that—stand, because stability is spiritual warfare!

The Reform:
Why "Rise, Grind, and Slay" Is Killing Your Business

"Rise, Grind, and Slay" sounds powerful on a mug, but it's a death sentence for Kingdom leaders. It glamorizes exhaustion, normalizes imbalance, and makes the idolatry of ambition look appetizing. *When grind becomes culture, innovation dies.* Creativity shrinks. Morale collapses. Burnout replaces brilliance. Here's why:

- You can't <u>innovate</u> when you're in survival mode.
- You can't <u>discern</u> when you're disconnected from rest.
- You can't <u>hear</u> strategy when you're drowning in stress.

What *feels* like productivity is often just panic with a planner.

<u>The Spiritual Framework</u>

Remember, you are Heaven's ambassador in that boardroom, hospital, lab, or job site. You were never sent there to fight like them. You were sent to *function* differently. While they grind, you <u>govern</u>. While they slay, you <u>strategize</u>. And while they burn out, you <u>build</u>. Because God's grace and mercy was always greater than grind. In Kingdom economy, sustainability *is Godly Success*. The greatest flex isn't how early you rise, but how deeply you rest in M-U-CCHHHHH FAITH; while Heaven works through you to create your Family's Succession Plan in the Earth.

- - - - -

 <u>Real Talk Reflection</u>:
- Where have I mistaken motion for momentum and exhaustion for excellence?
- Which part of my current assignment have I tried to manage through hustle instead of Heaven's strategy?

- What toxic system—corporate, cultural, or internal—keeps demanding performance when God is calling me to presence?
- Have I confused "being needed" with "being called"?

—Shift Statement:

- I don't belong to grind culture—I govern by grace.
- I'm not proving; I'm <u>positioning as my Father's Theocratic Arsenal.</u>
- I don't wrestle for what Heaven already ruled in my favor.
- I rise through prayer, build with clarity, and move with precision born from peace.
- My strength is strategy, not strain.
- My power is presence, not overwhelm.
- And my excellence flows from obedience, not overextension.

—Activation Exercise:

1.) Audit Your Arena: Write down the three environments where you spend the most time: workplace, ministry, and home. Identify which one most tempts you to over-perform or prove your worth. *(For me personally, I remember a point in time when it was ALL three. I used let people place UNREALISTIC Expectations on me in all arenas. I didn't want to EVER be deemed as lazy, NOW, call me whatEVER you want lol.)*

2.) Establish One System of Sabbath: Choose a recurring block of time each week *(even two hours)* when you silence notifications, emails, and demands. **YES,** on your Microsoft TEAMS *Guard it like a contract.*

3.) Set a Governance Alert: At the start of every major meeting or project, pause and ask: *Am I building from rest or reaction?*

4.) Document & De-stress: Create a "Justifications Folder" or "Work Diary" in your files. Store project outcomes, accolades, and clear data there. When accusation or gaslighting comes, you'll respond with evidence, not emotion.

5.) Pray the Exchange: Each morning this week declare: "Father, I exchange grind for grace, striving for strategy, and pressure for peace. I govern today by Your rhythm, not mine."

Chapter 7 — The Know-Like-Trust Factor: When Familiarity Replaces Responsibility, Credibility & Authority

Earlier this year, if you remember, I launched *Boss Mode Deconstructed* back in February at the leading of the Holy Spirit. Then, in July, He started talking to me about something that honestly made me raise an eyebrow—the **Know-Like-Trust Factor**.

Now, if you've ever sat in a marketing meeting or scrolled through an entrepreneur reel, you've heard it: *People only buy from those they know, like, and trust.* Cute, right? It sells workshops and hashtags. But when God said it to me, He wasn't talking about conversion rates—He was talking about *Kingdom conversion.*

So, I said, "Okay, Lord, help me understand this," and He replied, *Daughter, what happens when the people like you, but they don't obey Me? What happens when the culture replaces My credibility with clout?* Whew. That's when I knew this wasn't going to be your average TED Talk.

Trendiness vs. The Blueprint

Everybody wants to be a boss, but not everybody wants to be governed. See, grind culture taught us that leadership means visibility. Heaven teaches that leadership means responsibility and accountability. Let me make it plain. In business, they tell you to "build your brand so people know, like, and trust you." But in the Kingdom, we don't *market ourselves; we mirror Christ*. Yes, people see you and we are to show ourselves to be friendly, aka character full and kind, but this doesn't mean that they have to like you or hangout or spend time outside of work. You are building a relationship while you work. Your work speaks for itself. You are interceding if they request it, your insight provided strategy, or solutions when led and when asked of them is helping build the right kind of relationship without setting yourself up with a Hammond. Ester was strategic.

If your "product" is Jesus, and your assignment is to call people higher; to repentance, to transformation, to excellence; then liking you is optional. You can trust me and still not like me, especially if my obedience convicts your comfort.

That's why I say all the time, some one trusting you and knowing that your are authentic, still won't necessarily make you popular.

And listen; half the time the voices trying to give you "strategy" didn't even read the Owner's Manual. Your cousin, your mama, and John from accounting can't tell you how to build what Heaven downloaded. I don't care how many vision boards y'all made together at brunch. Unless God signed the blueprint, it's just décor.

When Know-Like-Trust Becomes Too Familiar

Here's where we mess up. We confuse *being relatable* with *being reachable.* Some people think "authenticity" means full access. They want to *de-robe* you so they can feel comfortable, then complain when they no longer feel covered. Or they all of a sudden need a "New Perspective" or "Fresh Eyes", because they are now out of "love" with you. Now they don't like you! They are overly familiar and don't trust the value that you bring. They cannot help to believe that you just cannot know this or have this right because they just had that virgin daiquiri with you at the company dinner party last week.

It happens everywhere—from the church pews to corporate boardrooms. One minute you're the go-to expert, the next you're "*just one of the team*" they can talk to any kind of way. *Familiarity creeps in, and respect walks out.* Let me be clear, it's not even always intentional.

I've seen it firsthand. In corporate spaces, I've watched colleagues cross professional lines because they mistook kindness for permission. They'd joke too loosely, talk around my leadership decisions, or treat my excellence like it was optional. And because I didn't want to appear "unapproachable," I let it slide.

That's how the enemy works. He won't always attack your assignment directly—he'll water down your authority through over-familiarity.

Authenticity
Without Over-Exposure

I'm not saying don't participate in the "team building exercises", but you bring the Apostolic Example of Authority with you when you go sit with Jo Smoo, John and Susan the friendly Gossip.Let me help somebody: transparency isn't telling everyone everything; it's telling the right people the right things in the right season.

Authenticity doesn't require you to strip down to prove you're real. Sometimes the most authentic thing you can do is protect what's still in progress.

Because here's the truth, once people become overly familiar, they stop listening. They start treating divine strategy like casual suggestion. And when that happens, you lose credibility, not because you lacked character, but because you let your guard down in the wrong crowd. In the church vernacular, baby they start treating you like you common. And let's be honest many of them already don't respect you in the first place. Protect the oil.

The Illusion of Authenticity
and My Wake-Up Call

I lived this. There was a season when I thought openness equaled obedience. I said yes to every meeting, every mentoring session, every call. I poured and poured until I had nothing left but fumes.

That's when my body shut down. Fatigue. Pain. Inflammation elevated. I had the warning signs all throughout my life, all throughout my career. I was ignoring all the discerned flags putting them off to do something for someone else. For a disrespectful client, a cut throat thieving boss, and a toxic culture.

I was preaching rest while ignoring it myself. I kept trying to be "available," because I didn't want to seem distant. But the truth is—I was dying under the weight of being *liked*. I would have never thought I cared about being liked…but when you prioritize you last, that's exactly what that said.

The world calls that "visibility." Heaven calls it *vulnerability without covering.* And that's dangerous. When the lines between authentic and over-exposed blur, your immune system, your mind, and your spirit all take the hit.

That health battle that none of us had a name for—the Early AxSpA, the inflammation, the weakness the temporary paralysis—taught me that familiarity can be fatal when boundaries are absent. It forced me to rebuild my rhythm around rest, privacy, and my D^3O.

The Reset:
Rebuilding Boundaries & Blueprint

Now I operate by a new Know-Like-Trust Factor: Know God. Like His Ways. Trust His Timing. That's the framework that *keeps me sane* and prophetically strategic, because baby I'm just a "little bit smart", and it's only because of Abba lol. I told you I like frameworks, this one helps me discern who deserves access and who just wants association. Don't get crazy or churchy undignified with me. I am an Analytical Seer, literally, the Bible is a WHOLE FRAMEWORK!

If you lead in business or ministry, write this down:

- Access should mirror assignment.
- Familiarity without responsibility is dysfunction.
- If they can't honor your boundaries, they can't handle your blueprint.

In corporate life, that means you document decisions, set communication protocols, and stay cordial but clear. In ministry, that means you love people deeply but don't let them idolize proximity. In personal life, that means you stop apologizing for protecting your peace.

The Reform
Responsibility Restores Respect

I used to think credibility came from visibility. Nope. Credibility comes from stewardship. It's proven over time, not performed on platforms. So, I stopped auditioning for rooms God already reserved. *I learned to guard my anointing like it's intellectual*

That's when my body shut down. Fatigue. Pain. Inflammation elevated. I had the warning signs all throughout my life, all throughout my career. I was ignoring all the discerned flags putting them off to do something for someone else. For a disrespectful client, a cut throat thieving boss, and a toxic culture.

I was preaching rest while ignoring it myself. I kept trying to be "available," because I didn't want to seem distant. But the truth is—I was dying under the weight of being *liked.* I would have never thought I cared about being liked…but when you prioritize you last, that's exactly what that said.

The world calls that "visibility." Heaven calls it *vulnerability without covering.* And that's dangerous. When the lines between authentic and over-exposed blur, your immune system, your mind, and your spirit all take the hit.

That health battle that none of us had a name for—the Early AxSpA, the inflammation, the weakness the temporary paralysis—taught me that familiarity can be fatal when boundaries are absent. It forced me to rebuild my rhythm around rest, privacy, and my D^3O.

The Reset:
Rebuilding Boundaries & Blueprint

Now I operate by a new Know-Like-Trust Factor: **Know God. Like His Ways. Trust His Timing.** That's the framework that *keeps* *me sane* and prophetically strategic, because baby I'm just a "little bit smart", and it's only because of Abba lol. I told you I like frameworks, this one helps me discern who deserves access and who just wants association. Don't get crazy or churchy undignified with me. I am an Analytical Seer, literally, the Bible is a WHOLE FRAMEWORK!

If you lead in business or ministry, write this down:

- Access should mirror assignment.
- Familiarity without responsibility is dysfunction.
- If they can't honor your boundaries, they can't handle your blueprint.

In corporate life, that means you document decisions, set communication protocols, and stay cordial but clear. In ministry, that means you love people deeply but don't let them idolize proximity. In personal life, that means you stop apologizing for protecting your peace.

The Reform
Responsibility Restores Respect

I used to think credibility came from visibility. Nope. Credibility comes from stewardship. It's proven over time, not performed on platforms. So, I stopped auditioning for rooms God already reserved. *I learned to guard my anointing like it's intellectual property—because it is*. And I realized that when you walk in divine authority, you don't have to beg for respect; your fruit will speak for you.

If people can't handle the version of you that's healed, whole, and governed—they weren't supposed to hold you anyway; and that goes for that *C-Suite Governance Call, that sister and brother with the platform, that intrusive friend,* or *that manipulating client.*

The next time someone says, "I thought we were cool," because you started enforcing boundaries, smile and say, "We still are. I just love you in order now."

Because *order protects oil.*

You were never called to make people comfortable. You were called to make Heaven visible. Don't trade your credibility for clicks, sales, promotions or your authority for applause. When you know who sent you, you don't need everyone to know, like, or trust you…just Heaven.

Real Talk Reflection:

- Where have I mistaken access for alignment?
- Who have I allowed too close who can't handle my call?
- Have I been transparent or just unguarded? Have I confused "being needed" with "being called"?

- What boundaries need to be rebuilt so my authority isn't diluted?

Shift Statement:
- I'm not called to be liked; I'm called to be light.
- I protect what Heaven placed in me by honoring boundaries and blueprints.
- I can be authentic without being accessible to everyone.
- Familiarity doesn't qualify people; fruit does.
- My credibility is rooted in character, and my authority is sustained by obedience.

Activation Exercise:
1.) **Access Audit:** Write down the five people or groups with the most access to you. Pray over each: *Is this covenant, seasonal, or sentimental?*
2.) **Boundary Blueprint:** Create three new rules for protecting your peace; one for work/business, one for ministry, one for family.
3.) **Authenticity Check:** Before you post, speak, or share, ask: *Does this reveal wisdom or just vulnerability?*
4.) **Health Reminder:** Schedule one act of rest this week. Protect your body as fiercely as your authority.

Chapter 8 — The Cost of Proving Yourself

Let me be real for a second; there's no promotion big enough to heal the wound that comes from needing to be seen. I had to learn that the hard way. For years, I was running on fumes trying to prove that I was *Enough*! Not because I didn't know who I was, but because I was surrounded by people who didn't.

You ever been there? You're overqualified, over-prepared, and underpaid — sitting in a meeting thinking, *Lord, they really don't see what You've built in me.* But you keep showing up anyway, smiling, documenting, performing, producing… all while *slowly dying* inside.

And the world claps for it. They call it "**grind**." They call it "**drive**." Heaven calls it disobedience wrapped in exhaustion. I refuse to drive another metric lol. I'll provide Strategy, I'll lead Implementation, but I will NOT force it down people's throats in the name of leading without authority and driving change or driving results.

I will not hold people's hands that have decided to be difficult and to kick off the prophetic word, in this case corporate strategy. God gives freewill with consequences and who am I to kill myself to undo a framework that He gave for Change Management in the earth. Shake the dust from off your Feet. That is Not Your Kingdom! And let this be your encouraging Moment: You Are STILL Operating in an Excellent Spirit!

Revelation Key I: Performance Is Not Proof

Let me tell you about the time I learned that lesson in full color. I was working on a corporate integration project that felt like a masterclass in insanity. I was leading deliverables across teams that didn't even *want* to be aligned, producing data and governance frameworks worth millions, and still being told, "You need to communicate better."

Now, what that really meant was: *You need to make us feel comfortable while we minimize your contribution.* What it really meant was: *We're threatened, but we'll repackage your ideas and call them ours.*

I was doing the work of twelve people without the authority, I had the title, not the pay. At every corner my team overall found ways to communicate that they *thought I was unqualified*, they thought I had a special role that they should have had themselves and to make these privileged colleagues feel better, leadership treated me like dirt in an attempt to make the greater team feel empowered". There was an issue for folks like me to be present in certain rooms and the audacity of us to even actually be taken seriously. I would intentionally NOT put all of my experience, certifications, qualifications on Meet the Team Bio Slides and use plain English as to not offend my team. I didn't want to bring unnecessary attention to myself when I needed these folks to "build bridges" to implement change management strategies and System Overhauls.

Over time, I stopped shrinking. I put my "Real Results" I stopped "Allowing My Manager to Claim Results, Architectural Builds and Trainings" I started using verbiage like *We are partnering* and then required her to partner. I stopped giving oil that heaven had not sanctioned and it began to tell the truth. My Fruit spoke. What happens when the Executives cannot deny your fruit but plausible deniability and optics are a real thing and they need you to keep being the fall guy. Well Heaven will back you up. And Sometimes we don't like how God will permit that action to manifest in your life.

And guess what? They *still* lied.

They took my work. They took my words. And when the results came in? Suddenly, no one could remember who wrote the plan that clearly had my name authored and dated all over it. Listen — Heaven took me to court on that one. Because I was crying about injustice, and God said, *"Jessica, I didn't ask you to prove yourself. I asked you to present evidence."*

Evidence is different. Proof is reactive; evidence is prophetic. Proof says, "Please believe me." Evidence says, "Watch the fruit." And that changed everything.

The Reset:
The Emotional Tax of Overperformance

Let's talk about the invisible cost of all that proving. When you're constantly overperforming, you start paying an emotional tax you didn't budget for. You start carrying guilt when you rest. You overthink emails. You replay conversations wondering if you sounded "aggressive" for simply being assertive. Every microaggression, every slight, every dismissal adds weight to your body and spirit.

I remember the day I realized I was literally sick from it. My body started shutting down. Pain, inflammation, fatigue — all the things that grind culture says to "push through." Long before that, I was recovering from a Mini-Stroke that was incorrectly diagnosed as an extreme reaction, then Hereditary Angio Edma, to back to square one year later, a Mini-Stroke at 37. I was having breathing issues all the time, now to know, last December they said Asthma. I had been on an inhaler for three years, but they could not figure out why. No one thought of sending me to a pulmonologist.

Why, because I was young. I was black, I was a woman. We can Handle ANYTHING according to many misinformed medical professionals. My cousin, rest her soul had been telling me that she felt that I needed to see a doctor since Christmas of 2022. I thought I was fine and would be fine. Come to find out She was right about it being an Auto Immune condition. I refuse to call it a disease, because God is Still a healer. That plus, wisdom, take the meds as necessary; ONLY those necessary, don't overdo. And NO GRINDING! I am learning at God's Pace. And Guess what, on God's Pace on my worst day, I'm still Excellent but I'm Healthy and Sustained by HIM.

They ruled out psychological, my job wanted it to be that and stress alone so bad so they could insinuate that I couldn't handle my job; shaking my head. I knew I was being attacked with a spirit of infirmity. I had been increasingly so from 2017, but I dismissed it then thinking it was me getting older. Me being pregnant with big babies. Me having gained too much weight. Marital Strain.

I started praying more and harder. I would pray, pray, pray. But you can't *pray your way through* what you *won't stop doing*. When your body starts responding to mistreatment, that's not weakness; that's data. Over-performance is a silent pandemic in leadership. We call it "being dependable," but what it really is… is a slow death by misplaced loyalty. I had to learn that silence wasn't weakness — it was strategy. Sometimes silence is the sound of Heaven building your witness file.

The Reform:
Stop Auditioning for Rooms Already Reserved

One of the greatest deliverances I've ever had was from the spirit of proving. I realized that I had been auditioning for rooms that Heaven already gave me keys to. If God says *you're chosen,* you don't need a callback. You don't need to perform your résumé into a promotion. You don't need to outwork dysfunction just to stay invited.

I started treating my work like a legal record — not a plea deal. When they stole my ideas, I documented it. When they disrespected my role, I documented it. But I didn't stop producing. I just stopped performing for approval. You can operate in excellence and still refuse exploitation. There were times when HR knew exactly what was happening. They knew about the gaslighting, the false narratives, the favoritism, the racism. But they protected politics over people. And yet, God whispered: *"You're not losing — I'm building your exit evidence."* That's the difference between quitting and graduating. *When you leave out of grace, Heaven promotes you in places paper trails can't reach.*

Corporate Realities, Kingdom Remedy

Now let's make this plain — here's how you handle it when culture tries to crush calling:

1. When your boss steals your work:
Don't spiral. Document. Keep your timeline, your deliverables, your proof. Then let the fruit speak. Because bitterness steals brilliance faster than betrayal ever could. *(We are talking about taking credit for what you did and spreading vicious lies that will harm your credibility, reputation to those in decision-making positions; i.e. that you aren't producing and that they are doing the majority of the work)*

2. When you're tokenized:
Stop shrinking. You are not the diversity initiative — you're the divine insertion. You weren't sent there to represent a quota; you were sent to model Kingdom excellence. The reality is you were <u>OVERQUALIFIED</u>, they just never told you, and Heaven knew and allowed you to find out AFTER HE placed you in the job. **God Qualifies the call.** Imagine not knowing you're Qualified and then finding out You are <u>OVERQUALIFIED</u>, then shrinking to FIT. <u>Foolery!</u>

3. When you're overlooked:
Stop begging for credit. Favor will outlast favoritism every single time.

4. When you're gaslit:
Stop over explaining. Create boundaries and keep receipts. Heaven hears what they said when you weren't in the room.

5. When your work environment turns toxic:
Don't match the dysfunction. Govern it. The safest place to be is in alignment — not agreement with chaos. Remember this:

when you are assigned, God will defend your record in rooms your voice never entered.

Revelation Key II: Proving Costs Too Much

Here's the truth that finally freed me: You can't be both exhausted and effective long-term. Heaven never asked me to *prove* my worth — it asked me to *preserve* my witness. And let me say this as your sister in both business and faith — proving will drain your creativity, your health, and your prophetic edge.

When you live to prove, you start performing instead of perceiving. And when you're performing, you stop hearing. That's how the enemy disarms leaders — not by disqualifying them, but by distracting them with the need to be believed. Don't chase validation. Steward visibility. Don't crave credit. Cultivate consistency. Because when you've been chosen, evidence follows you. You don't prove chosen—you *perform from purpose*.

There's a difference between proof and presence. Proof drains: presence governs. When Heaven calls you, your results don't need defending—they'll just start multiplying. Stop proving. Start producing. The fruit will always testify.

— — — —

Real Talk Reflection:

- Where have I overperformed to earn what God already gave?
- Who benefits from my silence while I'm suffering?
- Have I mistaken favor for free labor?
- What areas of my life need to stop auditioning for acceptance?

 Shift Statement:

- I no longer audition for validation.
- I work from purpose, not pressure.
- My receipts are spiritual, and my excellence is eternal.
- I produce from peace, not panic.
- I am Heaven's evidence, not Earth's employee of the month.

 Activation Exercise:

1.) **Proof vs. Purpose Audit:** List three areas where you've been proving instead of partnering. Ask: "Did God assign this, or did I assume it?"

2.) **Favor Folder:** Start keeping a record of outcomes, wins, breakthroughs, and testimonies—evidence of your brilliance and excellence without exploitation.

3.) **Exit Grace Plan:** If you're in a toxic environment, create your transition strategy with prayer and documentation.

Don't announce your exit—prepare for it. Grab a Copy of my Analytical Pioneers Book and Workbook or get on the Waitlist!

4.) Prayer of Release:
"Father, I release the burden of proving myself to people You never told me to please. I rest in the evidence You've already written about me. Make my fruit undeniable and my peace unshakeable. In Jesus' name, Amen."

Chapter 9 — Authenticity in Weakness When Transparency Becomes a Weapon and a Witness

Let me start here: **Yes, I broke down —but I didn't bow out.** I didn't crumble because I lacked faith. I didn't break because I was out of alignment with my spiritual metron. I crashed because I kept confusing *capacity* with *calling*. I thought saying "yes" to every assignment proved loyalty. What it really proved was that I hadn't yet mastered the art of *holy boundaries.*

There came a moment when I couldn't fake strength anymore. My body was screaming, "Sit down somewhere!" and Heaven was echoing it. I'd be on conference calls with a heating pad, leading strategy meetings with pain behind my ribs, and smiling through a camera lens while whispering, *"Lord, please let this call end before the next flare hits."*

But here's what I learned: **weakness isn't disqualification; it's divine data**. Every limitation reveals where God wants to show up stronger.

The Revelation:
Power Perfected in Weakness

Corporate culture trains you to posture: to hide the limp, fix the smile, and deliver on time no matter what's happening behind the scenes. The world claps for composure. Heaven applauds surrender. When Paul said, "My grace is sufficient," he wasn't writing a devotional—he was documenting a case study in leadership under pressure. God didn't remove his thorn; He gave him revelation inside it.

That's me. That's many of you. Leading teams while healing. Delivering excellence while depleted. Still hearing God in boardrooms while your body begs for rest. I used to pray, "Lord, make me unstoppable." Now I pray, "Lord, make me unshakable." Because unstoppable *sounds sexy*—until you realize it means *you never stop long enough to breathe*.

The Reset:
Rebuilding After the Break

When my diagnosis came—Early AxSpA a derivative of Parent, Early Anklylosing Spondylitis: inflammation, fatigue, nerve pain; it forced me to confront something deeper than disease: identity like I was led to do in *The 40-Day Onslaught.*

Who was I without constant output? Who was I if I couldn't meet every deadline or attend every meeting? I discovered the version of me Heaven wanted didn't need performance metrics; she needed permission to heal. So, I rested. I cried. I un-subscribed from hustle. Go to therapy if necessary! I started walking, stretching, breathing, and listening.

I stopped answering every call that began with, "I know you're busy, but..." and started messaging those that really just wanted to pimp some free information out of me or wanted to borrow funds...lol Ironically, many of those calls stopped too once folks knew I was out of work but increased around birthdays.

Slowly, strength came back—not the kind that hustles, but the kind that holds peace.

The Reform:
Redefining Strength

The world defines strength as *never flinching.* Heaven defines it as *never faking.* Authenticity in weakness means you can say, "I'm still healing, but I'm here." It means you can delegate without guilt and still deliver results. It means you stop competing with people's perception of what strong should look like.

In Pharma, in leadership, in ministry, I've learned that vulnerability doesn't diminish authority—it deepens it. You gain more credibility by telling the truth about the journey than pretending you floated through it untouched. Transparency is not over-sharing; it's precision sharing. You give people the wisdom, not the wound. You model what redemption looks like in real time.

Revelation Key
<u>Your Limp Is Leadership</u>

Every leader has a limp. Yours might be visible; mine showed up in medical records and missed moments. But the limp was proof that I wrestled and still came out blessed. Thank God I didn't have to keep the limp. There are moments during a flare state that I see it show up from time to time. So, what should you do in real life?

You STOP hiding your humanity behind your heroism. Stop apologizing for needing rest, therapy, or retreat. Even Jesus withdrew to pray. If the Son of God needed a Sabbath, so do you. Weakness invites God into spaces we keep trying to decorate for people. Let Him dwell there and then you too ABIDE!

Your strength isn't in how much you carry; it's in how quickly you surrender it all. Authenticity in weakness isn't about falling apart in public; it's about refusing to perform in private. Let your limp lead. Let your transparency teach. And let your healed humanity become Heaven's loudest sermon.

Real Talk Reflection:
- Where have I mistaken perfection for strength?
- What pain have I been managing instead of healing?
- Who am I trying to impress by pretending I'm okay?
- How has God been asking me to slow down so He can restore me?

 Shift Statement:
- I no longer hide my humanity; I honor it.
- My weakness is not a liability; it's a landing place for grace.
- I trade performance for presence.
- I lead from scars, not from stress.
- I'm not trying to be unstoppable; I'm learning to be unshakable.

 Activation Exercise:

1.) **Write Your Weakness Inventory:** List the areas where fatigue, fear, or frustration still linger. Next to each, write how God has shown Himself strong there.

2.) **Schedule a Sabbath Moment:** One day this week, block two hours of uninterrupted rest. No emails, no texts; just silence, worship, or journaling.

3.) **Tell One Truth Publicly:** Share one authentic story or testimony that shows how God met you in weakness. Let it serve others, not seek sympathy.

4.) **Pray for Perspective:**

"Father, thank You for trusting me with a testimony that proves Your strength. Teach me to lead honestly, to rest boldly, and to show others that wholeness is not the absence of weakness; it's the awareness of Your presence in it. In Jesus' Amen."

Part III
The Blueprint
Healing the Leader Within

Chapter 10 — The Apostolic Charge: Gracious Mercy Over Grind

Somewhere between deliverables and destiny, Heaven asked me a question that changed my life: **"Now that you've survived the system, can you steward it differently?"** That's the real call of the apostolic reformer. Not to abandon culture, but to rebuild it. To take the blueprint Heaven downloads and translate it into heavenly downloaded processes, principles, and people who function by governance, not grind.

Welcome, you are almost ready for **Kingdom Economics** after you heal of course! (*I'm working to finish it up!*)

This isn't the end of *Boss Mode Deconstructed*; it's the beginning of your rebuild.

The Revelation
Apostolic Resilience

I've learned that reform doesn't begin in a boardroom; it begins in recovery. You can't govern what you haven't healed from. That's why *The 40-Day Onslaught* had to happen first . It wasn't punishment; it was preparation. It stripped me down so that what I build now can stand.

Apostolic Resilience is Heaven's antidote to burnout. It's the divine ability to rebuild after every storm without losing your softness, your discernment, or your discipline. It's leading while healing, but this time from a place of grace.

Grace doesn't erase structure; it governs it. Grace brings strategy, sustainability, and sanity back to leadership.

The Reset
From Survival to Strategy

Let's be honest: we learned how to survive systems that were never built for us. But survival isn't the same as stewardship. The Kingdom isn't calling for survivors anymore; it's calling for architects.

You're not just a leader, you're a *blueprint carrier.* Your scars are measurements. Your lessons are foundations. Your obedience is the permitting process for the next generation. When Heaven rebuilt me, He said, *"This time, we're not building for applause — we're building for inheritance."*

That's when I started documenting differently. I stopped writing memoirs of pain and started drafting manuals for purpose. That's how *The 40-Day Onslaught Devotional* and *Analytical Pioneers Book Set* were born — as blueprints for anyone ready to heal the leader within and pioneer legacy without losing their soul.

The Reform
Governance Over Grind

We don't drive for results; we implement God's plan. We don't hustle for honor; we steward His order. That's what Apostolic Leadership looks like in this era.

If you lead teams, families, ministries, or nations, hear me clearly: Grace is the new governance model. Grace flows in systems, not sentiments. It builds calendars that breathe. It restores the Sabbath to strategy. It teaches executives to prophesy before data, through data and through implementation of the design.

The next wave of Kingdom leadership isn't just spiritual — it's strategic. Prophets who can write policy. Intercessors who can run budgets. Analysts who can discern. Leaders who can legislate Heaven's will on Earth. This is what the *Analytical Pioneers* series is about — training seers, builders, and innovators to lead in both the boardroom and the prayer room without compromise.

The Blueprint
Healing the Leader Within

Before you build nations, build nervous systems that can handle the next miracle. Before you pioneer legacy, let God recalibrate your logic and your lifestyle. That's what healing the leader within looks like…

You can't pour prophetic vision into an unhealed vessel. So, *Enduring the Onslaught: 9-Month Devotional* and *the 40-Day Onslaught Journal* isn't just reading; it's restoration. It walks you through warfare, wisdom, and wellness one day at a time until your rhythm matches Heaven's again. The devotional heals your hearing.

The Analytical Seers Trilogy — The Journey from Obscurity to Visionary Insight, Marketplace Disruptors, and *Break Forth & GOFORTH!* A prophetic, practical series equipping leaders to see, speak, and build with Heaven's precision.

Analytical Pioneers trains your seeing and gives you tools to build. Together they position you to build wealth that worships — structures that bless bloodlines. Because generational wealth isn't just money; it's mastery. It's knowing how to multiply purpose without multiplying pain. It's raising families who build systems that outlive them.

That's the real inheritance! *A healed leader who births a healed lineage.*

Revelation Key
<u>Your Legacy Is the Lesson</u>

Your legacy isn't just what you leave behind; it's what you leave built. Every healed leader becomes a generational architect. Every surrendered assignment becomes a seed. The same God who brought me through burnout, betrayal, and boardrooms is now birthing blueprints through me. He's doing the same for you.

This is your commissioning moment. You've learned to rest, to govern, to discern, to delegate, to obey. Now it's time to build — healed, whole, and wealthy in wisdom. You've deconstructed the grind. You've rebuilt the rhythm. Now walk out the blueprint.

Heaven's HR has stamped you: "*Cleared for Construction.*" Go build legacies that look like the Kingdom, one healed leader, one healed lineage at a time.

Signed,
One of Heaven's Process Validation
& Structural Engineers

Epilogue Prose | Cleared for Construction

When I first started writing *Boss Mode Deconstructed,* I thought I was documenting pain.
Turns out, I was documenting proof.
Proof that purpose doesn't die in pressure.
Proof that Heaven can rebuild you right in front of the same people who underestimated you.
Proof that grace is still the strongest business model ever created.

This book wasn't written from a place of perfection —
it was written from process.
It was written from hospital beds, healing seasons, hard meetings, and holy moments where I thought I'd lost my rhythm, only to discover I'd found God's.

Every page was an altar.
Every revelation, a recalibration.
And now that you've read it, I pray you feel the same unshakable peace I found in surrender.

You don't have to grind to prove you're called.
You don't have to over-perform to prove you're anointed.
You don't have to trade your humanity to demonstrate holiness.

You just have to flow.
Rest.
Listen.

And then, build.
AMEN!

Because *Boss Mode Deconstructed* wasn't just a book about leadership. It's a spiritual manual for leaders like you who were born to reform culture, pioneer new systems, and govern from grace.

Heaven's HR already cleared you for the next project. Now you get to go forth, not in exhaustion, but in excellence. Not in ambition, but in alignment. Not to prove, but to pioneer.

And when you're ready to go deeper, meet me in the next blueprint —
where healing meets strategy, and legacy meets obedience. It took years for me to give birth to all of these. The journey has not been easy, but it's been worth it!

Available Now or Coming in 2026!!!

For Healing:
- *The 40-Day Onslaught: Before the Miraculous Divine Elevation*
- *A 9-Month Devotional for Breakthrough and Refinement*
- The *40-Day Devotional Journal*

For Emotional Healing & Reclaiming Your Voice:
- *Misfits: Finding My Voice*
- *Misfits: The Miracle Revealed*
- *Misfits: A 31 Day Journey to Revealing the Miracle of YOU!*

For Generational Planning:
- *Analytical Pioneers* — The framework for building wealth that is formed in worship to the Lord's statues and legacy that lasts.

To Stretch Your Faith:
- *A Superhero Ain't Nothing but a Sandwich (Adult Edition)* — A journey of identity, resilience, and supernatural renewal.

To Heal Your Marriage:
- 💍 *Mastermind YOUR Marriage!* —

   Kingdom communication, covenant strategy, and emotional restoration for couples who still believe.

Final Prayer

Father, thank You for every reader, builder, and believer who made it this far. Let their hearts align with Your strategy. Let their rest become revelation. And let their leadership become legacy. In Jesus' name, Amen.

CLEARED for BUILDING and CONSTRUCTION!

AFTERWORD

by Lillie A. Hill
Boss Mode Deconstructed: How the Diabolical Grind Culture Is Killing You and Your Business

As I turned the final page of BOSS Mode Deconstructed, I realized that this wasn't just a book; it was a direct order from the Holy Spirit commissioning me and other like-minded souls to move forward. Have you ever read a book that read you right back? Besides the Bible, no other book has delved into the recesses of my being and shined a light on my hidden places. This life manual came at the perfect time for me as I was entering the final phase of a sabbatical from work due to burnout. Each chapter reached deep into my soul and revealed principles that I had been struggling with for some time. Jessica not only reveals the corporate/ministry/life issues that we often face, but she also expertly guides the reader to move from the culture of hustle and grind towards growing with grace.

Readers will transition from burnout to blueprint, experiencing a transformation that can only be accomplished by such a visionary leader as Jessica. This project impacted me in every chapter. I was able to see how others have gaslighted me into overperforming, overproducing, and thus overworking. Reading this enlightened work brought to light the methods others used to define my competence and subsequently attempted to limit my growth. However, after reading "Deconstruction of Boss Mode," neither my performance nor my life will be the same. Jessica has given a clear call to those of us in leadership, whether in the four walls of the church or the marketplace. We are called to reform the culture through governance, healing, and wholeness.

However, we do not accomplish this in isolation; there's help. Jessica provided us with the supernatural blueprint for success. By integrating the principle of **D^3O** (Delegating, Discernment, Divine Timing, and Obedience), readers will not only re-energize themselves but will rejuvenate all areas within their own spheres of influence.

A Blessing as You Journey Forward:

As you move forward, it's time to reclaim the term BOSS Mode. A new definition has been established in the heavenlies. Simply know that you have everything that you need. The pain that you have endured has become power; the healing that you have claimed has prepared you for your next. Now standing ready to build, create, and leave a legacy, remember your template **D³O** as a tender guide. May you build with intention, rest without guilt. May you BOSS with compassion and maintain boundaries with grace. May you transform others through fullness of heart instead of emptiness of soul, from grace-given performance rather than manmade proving. May your legacy flow from a place of authenticity and not forced acceptance. You are ready, you are worthy—you are commissioned.

Next Steps:

The Boss Mode Deconstructed is not the end, but the foundation for a generation of healed, strategic, and spiritually aligned leaders. To continue developing the BOSS inside all of us, Jessica has added more weapons to her arsenal. Be on the lookout for her future works: *The 9-Month Onslaught Devotional and 40-Day Onslaught Journal*, *Analytical Seers Trilogy*, and *Analytical Pioneers* set.

ACKNOWLEDGEMENTS

First, to my Heavenly Father, my CEO, my Architect, and my Chief Strategist, thank You for trusting me with this assignment. For every word You whispered, every revelation You rebuilt, and every reminder that grace outperforms grind. You let me deconstruct the chaos and reconstruct the Kingdom; starting within me. To Jesus, my intercessor and blueprint. And to Holy Spirit, my divine project manager, You never let me submit drafts You didn't first edit in secret. Thank You for the divine rewrites. **My God is ONE!**

To my family, who held me together when I was rebuilding from the inside out; especially my husband and children. You endured deadlines, flare days, and "one more paragraph" nights. You are my proof that love is legacy.

To my spiritual covering community and leadership family and spiritual peers, thank you for discerning the call, confirming the commission, and protecting the oil when I couldn't see clearly. To my apostolic and prophetic mentors who called out the architect in me; your words became bricks in this foundation.

To my **Empower Me Enterprises** and **Empowered to Heal Ministries International** teams, thank you for believing in what Heaven spoke through me when it was still blueprints and battle plans. You didn't just help build this book; you helped build the systems it stands on.

To every reader, reformer, and Analytical Seer or Analytical Pioneer who will ever pick up this book, you are the reason I fought to finish. You are proof that obedience births more than books; it births movement.

And finally — to every leader who's ever cried in silence while holding up systems that didn't see your value, this one's for you. May this book give you permission to rebuild at Heaven's pace, to rest without regret, and to rise without resistance.

You are cleared for construction.

With love,
Jessica AA Highsmith
Apostolic Architect | Analytical Seer | Kingdom Builder

About the Author

Jessica AA Highsmith is a Prophet, Seer, and Apostolic Marketplace leader, widely recognized as a Nabi-Seeing Pioneer. Commissioned into the office of the prophet in 2022, she carries a unique dual mantle of prophetic clarity and apostolic strategy. Her assignment is to equip leaders to dismantle demonic systems, establish God's legacy, cultivate Kingdom wealth, and advance transformation across ministry, marketplace, and media.

Jessica is the author of *The Analytical Seers* trilogy, the upcoming *Analytical Pioneers* duet, *The 40-Day Onslaught Before the Miraculous Divine Elevation*, the *MISFITS* series, and more. She also contributed to the anthology: *Called, Crowned, Commissioned* with (Visionary: Dr. Dionne Greaves).

She is the Visionary of **Empowered to Heal Ministries International, Inc.**, which birthed the *Appointed Experiences Hub for Apostolic and Prophetic Leaders* and the **WCKW (Women Cultivating Kingdom Wealth)** Movement. Additionally, she is the Founder of **Empower Me Enterprises, Inc.**, a faith-based digital business and publishing boutique merging Kingdom insight with strategic innovation.

Through these platforms, Jessica develops Analytical Seers and pioneering leaders who bridge tears, warfare, and Kingdom strategy for lasting impact and legacy establishment. She also champions women and families in cultivating Kingdom wealth in every area of life through the vision of *Chayil Women.*

Visit:
> Www.JessicaAAHighsmith.com
> Www.EmpowerMeEnterprises.com
> Www.EmpowerMeBooks.com
> Www.AppointedExperiences.com
> Www.E2HM.international

- THE 40-DAY ONSLAUGHT: Before the Miraculous Divine Elevation
  ISBN: 978-1954418271

- Resilient Through the Onslaught: A 40-Day Journal for Breakthrough
  ISBN: 978-1954418332 PENDING

- Enduring the Onslaught: A 9-Month Devotional for Breakthrough and Refinement
  ISBN: 978-1954418349 PENDING

- Analytical Seers 1: The Journey from Obscurity to Visionary Insight
  ISBN: 978-1954418288

- Analytical Seers 2: Marketplace Disruptors
  ISBN: 978-1954418295

- Analytical Seers 3: Break Forth & GOFORTH! The Journey of a Nabi-Seer from Struggle to Victory, Healing, and Breakthrough
  ISBN: 1954418301

- MISFITS: Finding Your Voice
  ISBN: 978-1517459109

- Misfits: The Miracle Revealed
  ISBN: 978-1979991506

- Misfits: A 31 Day Journey to Revealing the Miracle of YOU
  ISBN: 1981708017

- Misfits: A 31 Day Journey to Revealing the Miracle of YOU
  Black & White Version
  ISBN: 978-1732773196

- A Superhero Ain't Nothing but a Sandwich (Adult Edition)
  ISBN: 978-1954418363 PENDING

- Not Another Vision Board Workbook
  ISBN: 978-1954418080

- MUSIC Healing & Breakthrough Songs:
  Orphan No More COPYRIGHT 2024

- MUSIC Healing & Breakthrough Songs:
  You Can Have It All COPYRIGHT 2024

- S.T.E.M. 4 Girls; The Urban Girl's Guide to the S.T.E.M.
  Disciplines
  ISBN: 978-1530231546

- A Superhero Ain't Nothing but a Sandwich (Teen Edition)
  ISBN: 1954418318 *(Contributing Author w/ Robert "RJ" Highsmith Jr.)*

- Nancy's Whimsical Journey: Embracing Your True Colors
  ISBN: 978-1954418264 *(Contributing Author w/ Josiah Isaiah Highsmith)*

- Noah's BIG Idea Journey: Becoming A Kid Ceo Blueprint
  ISBN: 978-1954418332 *(Contributing Author w/ Noah Lee Highsmith)*

- The Jots & Tittles of Scribes and Storytellers: Volume III
  ISBN: 978-0998073446 *(Anthology Contributing Author)*

- Made To Lead Millions Mandate
  ISBN: 8364655318 *(Anthology Contributing Author)*

- Called to Intercede: Volume One
  ISBN: 8776655111 *(Anthology Contributing Author)*

- Called Crowned Commissioned
  (Anthology Contributing Author)

NOTES

CH1 NOTES

CH1 NOTES

CH2 NOTES

CH2 NOTES

CH3 NOTES

CH3 NOTES

CH4 NOTES

CH4 NOTES

CH5 NOTES

CH5 NOTES

CH6 NOTES

CH6 NOTES

CH7 NOTES

CH7 NOTES

CH8 NOTES

CH8 NOTES

CH9 NOTES

CH9 NOTES

CH10 NOTES

CH10 NOTES

www.ingramcontent.com/pod-product-compliance
Lightning Source LLC
Chambersburg PA
CBHW061943220426
43662CB00012B/2010